BASEBALL IS BACK

for Ella and Nora with love...

by Michael Turner

Dear Ella and Nora, you're old enough now
to hear more about why we say, "Holy Cow!"

America is Baseball, a game that I love
since the time I broke in my very first glove.

Here are some memories and rules of the game.
Perhaps you will love it like me—just the same.

And maybe you won't or maybe you will.
I will love you the same, yes, I'll love you still.

Baseball is Back, when the birds announce Spring.
After Winter has warmed, there is hope that brings

a reason to cheer from any seat in the park,
when daddies let kiddos stay up way after dark.

Baseball is Back for the young and the old
in July's steamy heat and October's cold.

Let's go to the park and bring your friend Sarah.
We'll talk of a catcher named Yogi Berra.

Many kids love going to games it is true,
to eat hot dogs, popcorn, and ice creams too.

But baseball is much more than snacking on snacks.
It's teamwork, hard work, and 400 foot jacks.

There's a diamond with players, 9 on each team,
with bullpens and dugouts where managers scheme

ways after 9 innings to have the most runs,
with Frank Robinson this was more easily done.

There's 3 outs to each frame, 3 strikes and 4 balls,
and Visitors bat at the top of them all.

ROBINSON FIELD

| 34 | P. TURNER | | 3B | .360 |

TEAM	1	2	3	4	5	6	7	8	9		R	H	E
VISITOR	1	0	2	0	1	1	0	0	1		6	8	1
HOME	0	0	0	0	0	0	2	3			5	10	0

The pitchers throw fastballs, curveballs, and sliders,
in order to strikeout folks named Duke Snider.

Catchers like Bench backstop balls from the mound
and dig up the knucklers that get lost in the ground.

They gun down runners trying to steal bases,
Except for Lou Brock who is off to the races.

First base is the first place a batter first goes.
The first baseman must always be on her toes.

Fielding grounders, pick-offs, and charging drag bunts,
a Lou Gehrig will keep your team in the hunt.

Second and Shortstop fresh up from Triple A
must learn to turn the 6-4-3 double play.

To take their place beside the hero Jackie,
they'll need all 5 tools and they'll need them snappy.

Third base is known as the corner that's hot,
at which Screaming line drives aren't easily fought.

Be careful you don't boot, botch, bobble, or flub,
or Rockford won't want you on their championship club.

Left, center, and right, fielders on their horse,
catching cans of corn as a matter of course.

In the Green Monster's shadow with Sox of Red
was the Splendid Splinter whose first name was Ted.

Warning tracks, foul poles, and fan interference,
flipping the shades can make all the difference.

Basket catch, snow cone catch, any catch really,
Clemente and Mick...Yaz's name is quite silly.

A Catfish, a Goose, or perhaps a Big Train,
with Nolan or Neikro, batters swing in vain.

With Koufax, Kershaw, or Gibson on the mound,
next stop on this ride is Cooperstown.

Now batting, that's maybe the toughest of all.
Much goes into hitting that aspirin ball.

Your stance in the box, choke up on the lumber?
Bases are loaded, make contact, don't blunder.

Eye on the ball! Pick your pitch! Protect the plate!
No Golden Sombrero for you, don't be late.

Watch the signs from third base, just maybe the squeeze?
Not this time slugger, swing as hard as you please.

There are all sorts of hitters, pull, switch, and spray.
Clutch hitter, power hitter, Say Hey Willie Mays.

A blooper, a chopper, a fluke hit will do,
Let's keep the line moving, we're only down two.

Next up is clean-up, a legend named Hank.
Once the Hammer goes yard, the pitcher is yanked,

to the showers to take a freezing ice bath,
Stan, Eddie, and Cool Papa all cut a wide swath.

You win if you have the most runs after 9.
If tied, extra innings no matter the time.

Hooray! Another victory sealed,
but not all of baseball is down on the field.

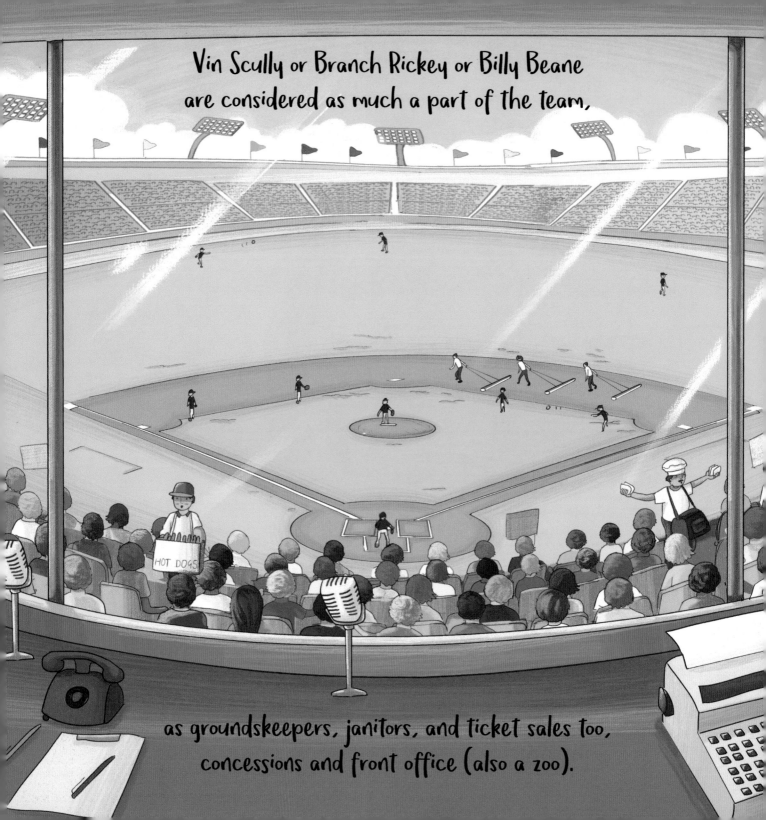

Chavez Ravine and Fenway have grace,
and maybe someday where Presidents race.

There is Wrigley, and there was one in New York,
the one that Ruth built, none of his bats were corked.

But it starts with T-ball and 2-4-6-8.
Team moms are the ones to appreciate.

Driving to practice and working too,
to encourage the sweet dreams of you know who.

Girls, that's some history and memories of mine,
rules and players from America's Pastime.
The game belongs to them, but also to you,
Baseball is Back, and there is nothing more true.

BASEBALL IS BACK

Baseball is Back

Copyright © 2013 by Michael Turner
First edition published in 2017

Artwork by: www.BookWorks.in & Michael Turner

Library of Congress Control Number: 2017901043

Turner, Michael. Baseball is Back / Michael Turner. -- 1st American ed.

Summary: Dad shares America's pastime with his daughters, by teaching them about baseball.

ISBN-13: 978-1542407779
ISBN-10: 154240777X

For more information, please contact:

Fuller & Rojo
PO Box 15361
Washington, DC 20003

Made in the USA
Columbia, SC
27 August 2018